INSIDE THE HINDENBURG

Text by Mireille Majoor
Illustrations by Ken Marschall

Additional Illustration by
Laurie McGaw and Donna Gordon
Historical Consultation by Dennis R. Kromm and John Provan

A MADISON PRESS BOOK
produced for
LITTLE, BROWN AND COMPANY

April 4, 1936

All 804 feet of its silver skin gleamed in the sunlight as the *Hindenburg* soared over Rio de Janeiro. In the giant airship's belly, travelers crowded around the open windows of the passenger quarters, cameras clicking furiously as they tried to get just the right shot of the breathtaking view over mountains, city, water, and sky. Below them sparkled the waters of Guanabara Bay. Just ahead, the rocky peak of Sugarloaf Mountain rose up from the waves.

Only four days before, the *Hindenburg* had taken off from Germany on its maiden voyage to South America. Its passengers were the first travelers to make the luxurious, non-stop journey across the Atlantic in the new zeppelin. No airplane yet built could fly across the ocean without stopping, and a voyage by ocean liner would have taken at least two weeks. But the *Hindenburg*'s passengers had made the crossing with speed and style in just three and a half days, sleeping in private cabins, eating in a spacious dining room, and relaxing in a comfortable lounge. Now, high inside their comfortable airborne hotel, they were floating over the coast of Brazil, sharing their view with the birds.

Werner Franz knew he was lucky. Times were so bad in Germany, even his father couldn't find work, but at fourteen, Werner already had a job with the Zeppelin Company. After flying three times from Germany to Brazil aboard the *Hindenburg*, Werner felt like a seasoned zeppelin crewmember. And tonight he was leaving for his first trip to America. He was a cabin boy now, but his dream was to become an airship

Luxury Liner of the Air

May 3, 1937

captain, in command of one of these graceful giants.

The year before, the *Hindenburg* had sailed over the Olympic Games in Berlin and every head in the stadium had turned to watch it float by. The huge swastikas on the *Hindenburg*'s tail fins were the emblems of the Nazi party, which had controlled the German government since 1933. The Nazis thought that a giant airship would be an excellent way to spread their message and had helped to pay for the *Hindenburg*'s

construction. In return, they could order the giant airship to make propaganda flights like the one over the Olympics.

Under their leader, Adolf Hitler, the Nazis had begun persecuting Jews and other minorities and suppressing freedom in Germany. The 1936 Olympic Games, held in Berlin, were meant to show the world the superiority of the German race. But Hitler's plan backfired when African-American athlete Jesse Owens won four gold medals and became the hero of the Games.

Up Ship!

May 3, 1937

Just a few more forks and he'd be finished. Werner wanted to make sure the tables in the officers' mess were set before the *Hindenburg* took off. The zeppelin's chief steward, Heinrich Kubis, had warned him that the flight would begin in half an hour. If Werner completed his duties before then, there would be enough time for him to race to the other end of the airship to his favorite seat by the small window in its nose. From there he could watch while the people, cars, and buildings on the ground below dwindled to dots as the zeppelin floated upwards. Werner straightened the jacket of his uniform. Soon they would be airborne.

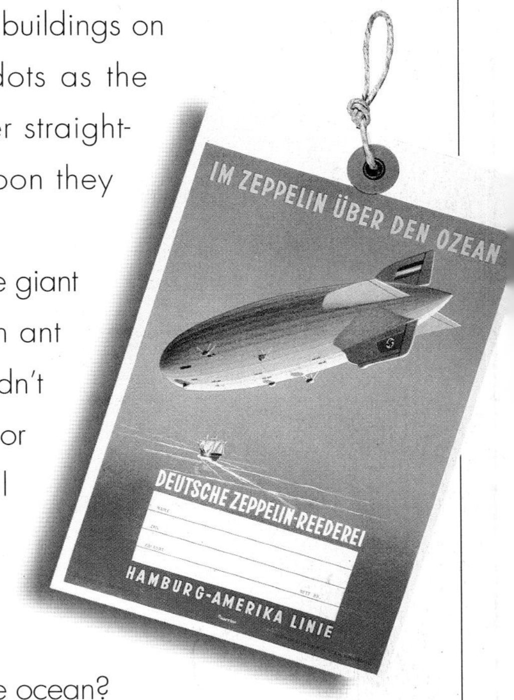

Outside, standing underneath the giant zeppelin, Irene Doehner felt like an ant looking up at an elephant. She couldn't tell where the *Hindenburg* began — or where it ended. Its vast silver hull curved up sixteen stories above her head and seemed to stretch out forever in either direction. This thing was going to carry her family over the ocean?

The Doehners had been visiting relatives in Germany and were flying to the United States on their way back to their home in Mexico. Irene was excited to be traveling on the *Hindenburg*. She had heard that last year's flights were packed with American movie stars, millionaires, newspaper reporters, counts and countesses, but the passengers lining up this evening looked disappointingly ordinary. Irene didn't recognize a single face. Still, the fact that this flight — the first to America of the 1937 season — was less than half full meant that she would have her own private cabin. Sixteen, after all, was too old to have to share with her parents or her two younger brothers, Walter, eight, and Werner, six.

(Left) The *Hindenburg* stands ready as its thirty-six passengers are escorted across the soggy landing field. A Zeppelin Company luggage tag, like the one shown above, was attached to every piece of their baggage.

IM ZEPPELIN ÜBER DEN OZEAN

DEUTSCHE ZEPPELIN-REEDEREI

HAMBURG-AMERIKA LINIE

Dropping water ballast from the airship (below) made it lighter so that it would rise more quickly at takeoff or descend more slowly at landing. Maneuvering the giant airship out of its hangar and across the landing field required a large ground crew (bottom).

(Right) Passengers crowd around the windows of the *Hindenburg* to wave at friends and family on the ground below. (Far right) A ticket for a 1936 flight from Lakehurst, New Jersey, to Frankfurt, Germany, shows that a zeppelin crossing cost $405.00 — about as much as the price of an automobile that year.

Boarding the *Hindenburg* was nothing like boarding an ocean liner. On a liner a porter took care of the luggage while the passengers simply strolled on board. But before an airship voyage, all passengers had to open their bags and wait while they were inspected. The Zeppelin Company stewards were looking for anything that might produce a spark or electric charge. Since the *Hindenburg* was inflated with hydrogen, one of the most flammable gases known, every step was taken to be sure that there was no possibility of fire. Camera flashbulbs, matches, and flashlights were pulled out and put aside. One of the stewards had even taken Mr. Doehner's cigarette lighter, explaining politely that it would be returned to him after they landed. "Just a routine precaution," smiled the steward. After all, in the more than twelve years that hydrogen-filled zeppelins had been carrying passengers, there had never been a fire.

The *Hindenburg* stood ready in a field just outside its hangar at Frankfurt airport. Even on such a rainy evening, people had gathered to watch the giant airship's launch. They stared at the *Hindenburg* and shook their heads in amazement.

The electric lights in the passenger quarters twinkled invitingly from the windows above her head as Irene climbed up the metal gangway into the zeppelin. At the top of the stairs she glanced at the bust of General Paul von Hindenburg, Germany's former president, for whom the airship was named. Two long corridors stretched out behind the General, each one punctuated by featherlight sliding doors that opened onto twenty-five passenger cabins.

By this time, the zeppelin had been unlocked from its mooring mast and was held on the ground by teams of men gripping thick ropes. On a command from the captain, they would let go the lines and set the airship free. A few minutes later, a cry of "Up ship!" rang out from the *Hindenburg*'s control car. At the signal, more than six hundred pounds of water stored in tanks inside the airship were dumped from the sides of the zeppelin. A group of spectators standing too close got caught in the sudden waterfall. They shrieked and sputtered, wringing the water from their coats. Laughing, the ground crew threw their ropes aside. Then, without so much as a shiver, the giant *Hindenburg* rose silently into the air.

The Hindenburg

It was the largest object ever to fly. Before airplanes could make a non-stop journey across the Atlantic, the *Hindenburg* carried passengers over the ocean with ease. The giant zeppelin was only 78½ feet shorter than the 882½-foot-long *Titanic*. Beside the *Hindenburg*, a blue whale, a blimp, and even a 747 jet look tiny.

Inside the 804-foot-long metal skeleton that gave the *Hindenburg* its graceful shape were sixteen enormous gasbags containing over seven million cubic feet of flammable hydrogen gas. This gas was what lifted the *Hindenburg* into the sky like a vast balloon and gave it the strength to carry an airborne hotel with room for fifty passengers in its belly. Four diesel engines — two on each side — powered the airship through the sky.

The *Hindenburg* was designed to be inflated with helium — a non-flammable lifting gas — but the American government, which controlled the world's largest supply of the gas, would not sell it to any other country. They feared that helium might someday be used for military purposes, such as inflating zeppelins that could be used for spy missions or for dropping bombs. So the Germans had to use flammable hydrogen gas in the *Hindenburg* instead. But because hydrogen has more lifting power than helium, the Zeppelin Company was able to add ten new passenger cabins, with room for twenty-two more passengers, to the *Hindenburg* in time for the start of the 1937 flying season.

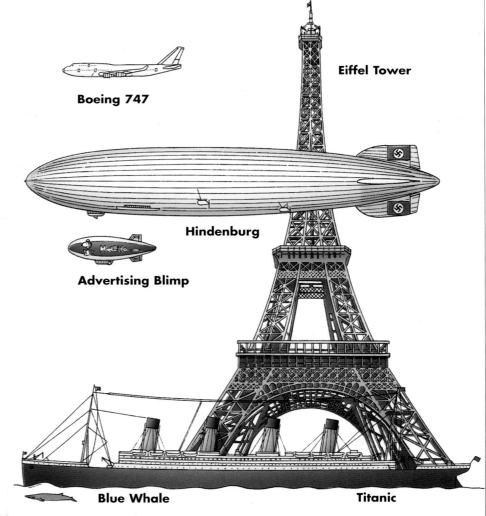

Boeing 747

Eiffel Tower

Hindenburg

Advertising Blimp

Blue Whale　　　　**Titanic**

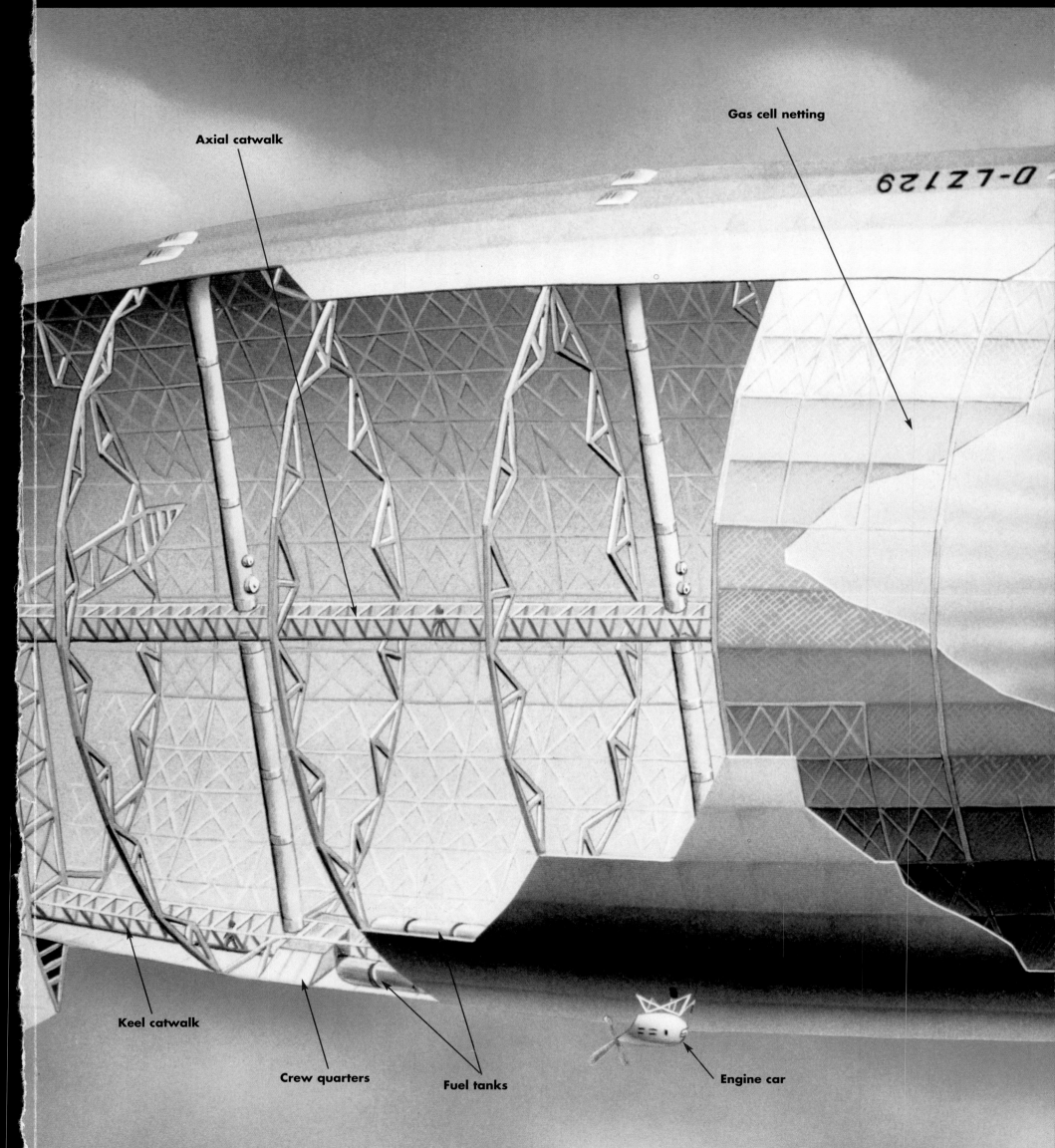

Gas cell netting

Axial catwalk

D-LZ129

Keel catwalk

Crew quarters

Fuel tanks

Engine car

Tail fin

Rudder

Elevator

Auxiliary control room

Landing wheel

Rooms with a View

The *Hindenburg*'s passenger quarters were located on two decks built inside the airship's frame. The top deck, A-deck, held twenty-five private cabins, each with two bunks. But A-deck's large, elegant public rooms were the place where passengers spent most of their time. Meals were served in a dining room with seating for up to fifty people. Afterwards, passengers could relax in the lounge. During the 1936 flying season, an aluminum baby grand piano weighing only 397 pounds was the star attraction here. Promenade decks nearly fifty feet long on each side of A-deck gave passengers a route for their strolls. The built-in seats beside the promenade's downward-sloping windows allowed travelers to watch the world pass by below them. (The *Hindenburg*'s captain always tried to fly the airship low enough to give passengers a good view of the scenery beneath.) Downstairs on B-deck passengers could use the toilets, lather up in the world's first airborne shower, or visit the airship's bar and smoking room, which stayed open until the last guest said good night. The kitchen, officers' mess, and crew's mess were off-limits to passengers.

A-Deck

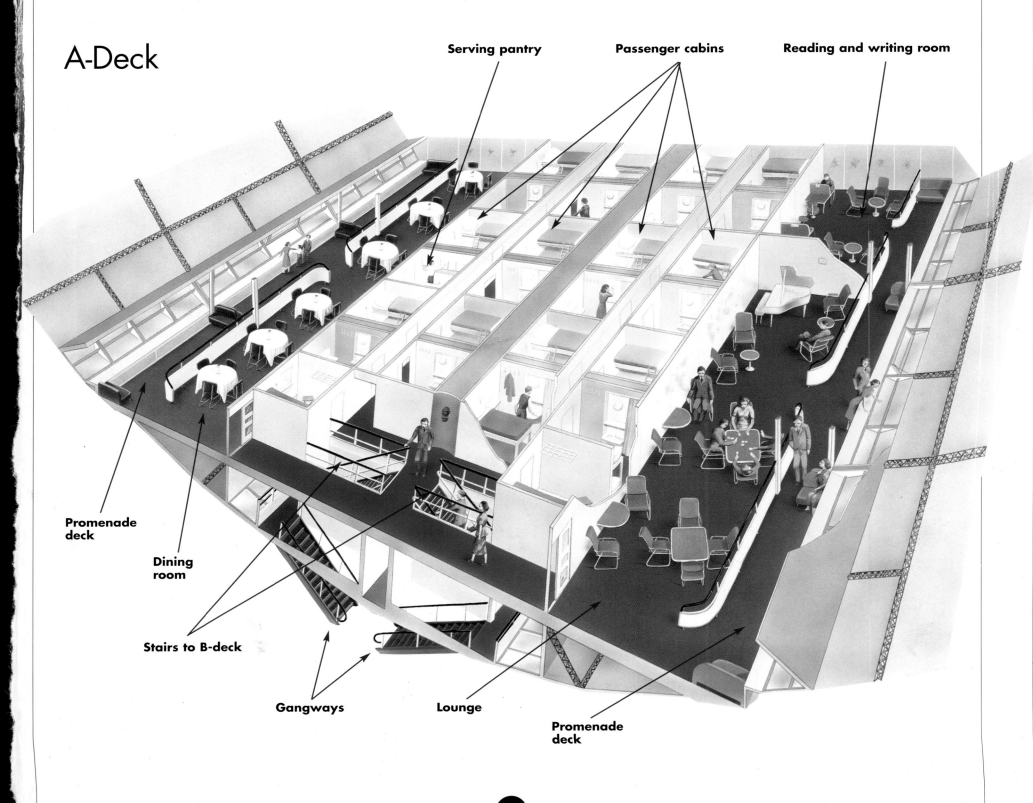

Serving pantry

Passenger cabins

Reading and writing room

Promenade deck

Dining room

Stairs to B-deck

Gangways

Lounge

Promenade deck

B-Deck

(Top) Meals aboard the airship were so relaxed that sometimes passengers arrived for breakfast in their pajamas. (Above) The baby grand piano the *Hindenburg* carried on all its 1936 flights made the lounge the most popular spot on the zeppelin. The piano was removed in 1937 to save weight.)

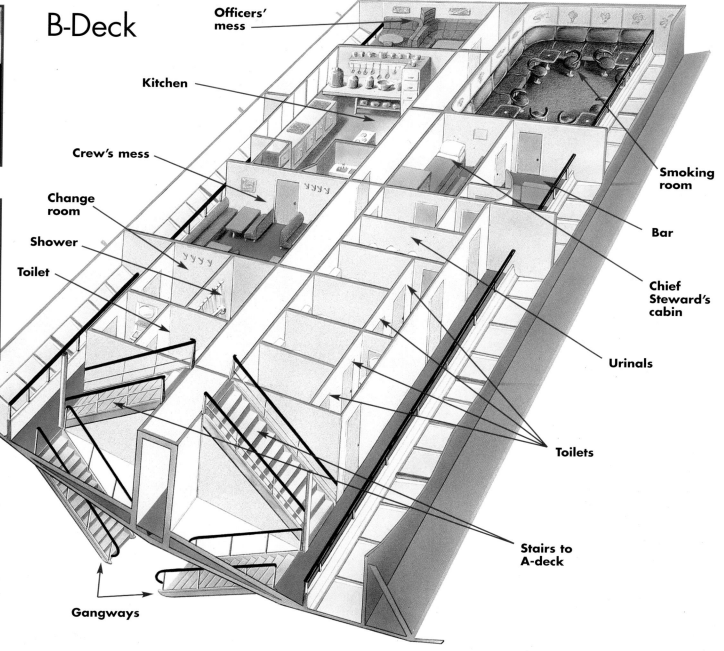

Officers' mess

Kitchen

Crew's mess

Change room

Shower

Toilet

Smoking room

Bar

Chief Steward's cabin

Urinals

Toilets

Stairs to A-deck

Gangways

Flying the Hindenburg

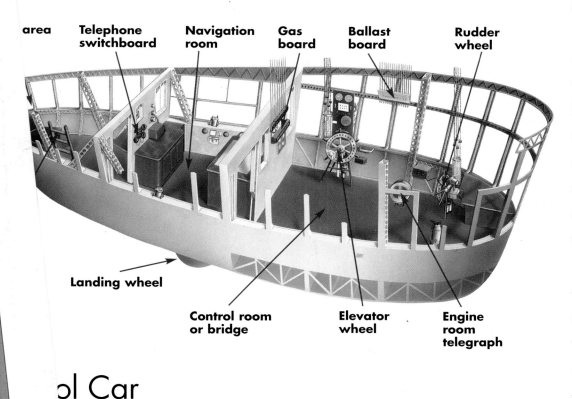

area

Telephone switchboard

Navigation room

Gas board

Ballast board

Rudder wheel

Landing wheel

Control room or bridge

Elevator wheel

Engine room telegraph

ol Car

The *Hindenburg*'s captain directed the airship's flight from the control car. Using the engine room telegraph, he could signal the mechanics aboard the zeppelin's four engine cars when he wanted to change speed. If he wanted the airship to go higher, he lightened it by releasing water ballast from the water tanks using the ballast board. If he wanted to lose altitude, he made the zeppelin heavier by releasing hydrogen from vents at the top of the airship. The gas board allowed him to check the level of gas in each cell.

Two crewmen were needed to steer the airship. A rudder operator steered left and right, using the vertical flaps on the airship's tail fins, while the elevator man had the vital task of ensuring that the airship — and everything in it — stayed level by adjusting the horizontal flaps.

The Hindenburg

The *Hindenburg*'s luxurious passenger quarters occupied only 20% of the space inside one of its sixteen giant gas cells. The rest of the zeppelin's interior was filled by enormous gasbags and the intricate framework of lightweight Duralumin rings and girders that gave the airship its shape.

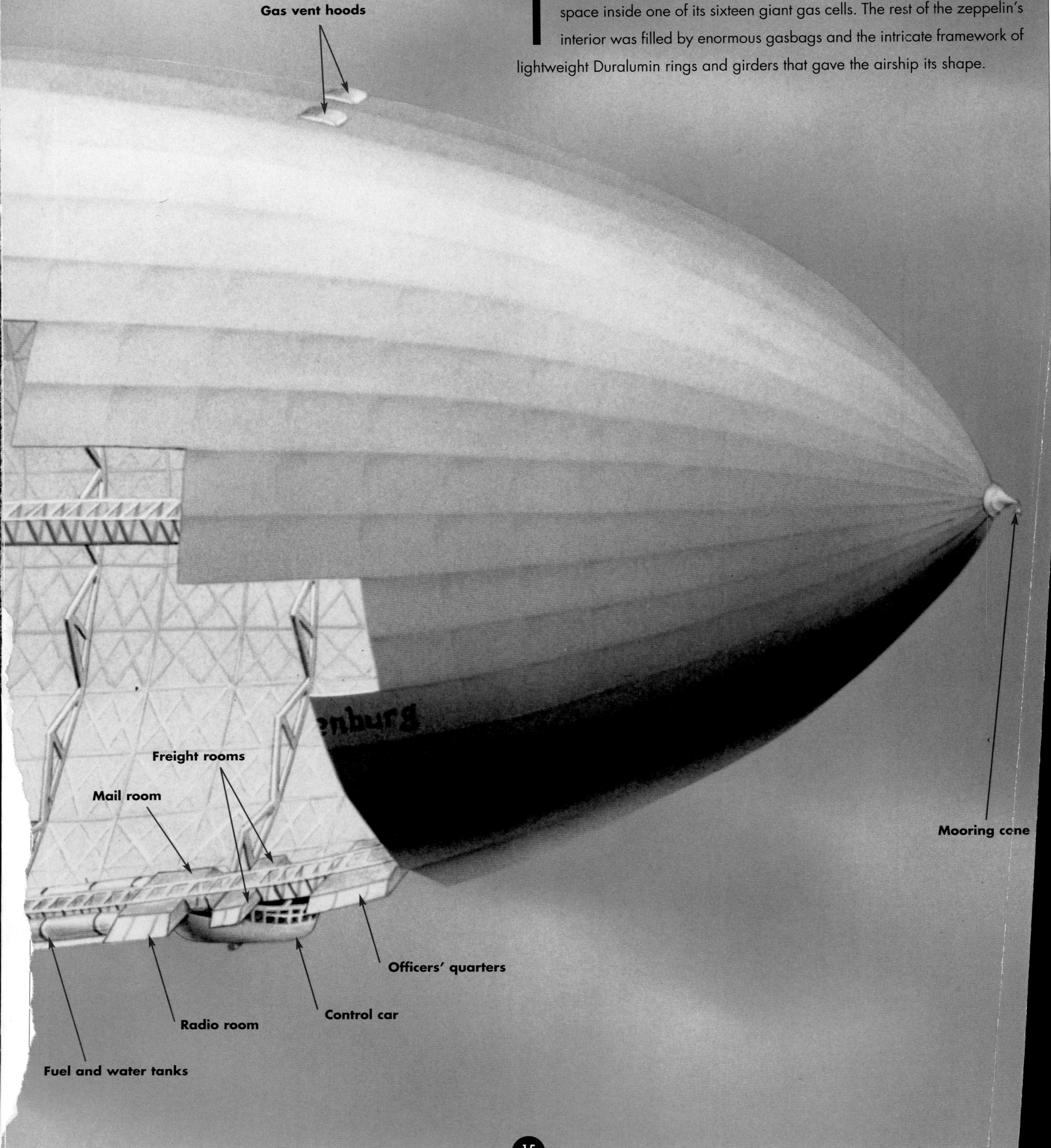

Gas vent hoods

Freight rooms

Mail room

Officers' quarters

Mooring cone

Radio room

Control car

Fuel and water tanks

Gas cell

Main frame

Bracing wires

Gas shaft

Fuel, oil, and
water tanks

Access walkway to engine car

Crew quarters

Passenger quarters

On Board

May 4, 1937

Irene opened one eye. What was that smell? The night before, after the zeppelin had taken off, she had hurried to her cabin, hung her dresses in the small closet, and stretched out on her bunk. She wanted to rest for a moment before meeting her parents in the dining room for a midnight snack. Somehow she must have fallen asleep. On a train or an ocean liner, she could always hear the chugging engines. But Irene hadn't heard a thing on the *Hindenburg*. Now she was sure it was morning. And she was sure she smelled baking.

On the deck below Irene, Werner Franz slipped another tray of hot rolls into the miniature elevator that would take them up to the passenger dining room on A-deck. It was amazing what airship travel did for people's appetites. This was the sixth tray of rolls he'd taken from the electric ovens that morning.

By the time Irene appeared in the dining room, the rest of her family was already finishing breakfast. Her father smiled as he poured her a cup of hot tea and passed her a fresh roll. Then, as he did after every meal, Mr. Doehner placed a packet of cigarettes on the table in front of him and patted his pockets in search of his lighter. Irene

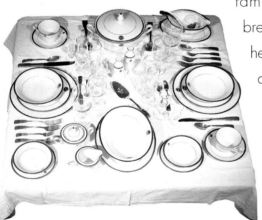

tried not to giggle. He must have already forgotten that he'd given it to the steward the night before. If he wanted to smoke, Irene reminded him, he'd have to go downstairs to the smoking room on B-deck. "Oh, of course. The smoking room," her father replied sheepishly.

Mrs. Doehner had been horrified when she learned that there was a smoking room on board the *Hindenburg*. After all, the zeppelin was kept aloft by hydrogen gas, one of the most flammable gases known. But the airship's stewards had explained that the air in that room was kept at a higher pressure to prevent any stray hydrogen gas from outside it leaking in and that the single lighter in the room was chained in place. The smoking room even had a

(Left) A table set with white and blue Zeppelin Company china. (Right) To prevent any hydrogen from seeping in, the smoking room was sealed off from the rest of the airship by an air-lock door. Behind this door, passengers could light up pipes, cigars, and cigarettes.

A Gallery in the Sky

The fabric-covered walls of the *Hindenburg*'s passenger quarters were decorated with handpainted artwork and every room had its own theme. Behind Irene on the wall of the lounge is a map of the world, showing the routes of history's most famous explorers and their ships. Mrs. Doehner addresses postcards in the reading and writing room beneath scenes

of the history of postal delivery. In the smoking room on B-deck, Mr. Doehner enjoys a cigarette — forbidden everywhere else on the zeppelin — while admiring artwork showing the development of lighter-than-air flight, starting with the first balloons and ending with the *Graf Zeppelin*, the most famous German airship before the *Hindenburg*. Looming out of sight over the passenger quarters is one of the airship's giant gas cells. The hydrogen gas inside it has risen to the top of the cell, leaving its bottom empty to billow and flutter.

For Crew Only

Werner (opposite) makes his way along the lower catwalk. (Right) He descends the ladder to the engine car. (Below) A mechanic's job was to

watch the engines, adjust their speed, and make any repairs. Mechanics worked in shifts, so that one of them was on duty in each engine car twenty-four hours a day.

fireproof floor and walls. "Accidents," she had been assured, "are not possible."

After her father left for the smoking room, Irene wandered across the airship to the lounge, a long, narrow room whose walls were decorated with a map of the world showing the routes of some of the greatest explorers. This room had the same long bank of windows as the dining room. Irene opened one and leaned out to breathe the fresh sea air. Hundreds of feet below her, the sun sparkled on the endless ocean, dotted with trans-Atlantic liners looking more like bath toys than ships carrying thousands of passengers. The *Hindenburg* had passed over Germany and northern Holland on its way to the ocean the night before. It wouldn't see land again until it reached North America.

Twelve o'clock. Time for Ulla's lunch. Stored in the cargo area of the *Hindenburg* were extra luggage, airplane parts, and Ulla von Heidenstadt, the German shepherd a passenger was taking home as a surprise for his children. Werner changed into a pair of felt boots with rubber soles — made without any metal parts that could create

dangerous sparks — tucked a bag of dog biscuits under his arm, and headed to the back of the airship.

The rear of the *Hindenburg* was off-limits to passengers (except for those on guided tours), but was constantly patrolled by crewmembers inspecting the gasbags, checking fuel and water levels, and repairing any tears in the silver fabric that covered the zeppelin's frame. Werner made his way along the narrow catwalk, surrounded by a forest of interlocking girders and dwarfed by the vast hydrogen-filled gas cells that loomed overhead. He felt like he was at the bottom of an enormous cave. Far above him he could see the axial catwalk, where the most sure-footed of the crewmen inspected the upper parts of the gasbags and the wires and netting that held them in place. If anything needed repair, they would be the first to know.

After he fed the dog, Werner met Richard Kollmer, one of the *Hindenburg*'s mechanics. The day before, Kollmer had promised him a tour of the engines, a part of the airship Werner had never seen. He strapped on the leather helmet Kollmer passed him to protect his ears and followed the mechanic to a small door on the side of the *Hindenburg*.

Werner's heart almost stopped when he stepped outside. The

wind whipped his face so fiercely he felt as if his skin might peel off. He reached back and gripped the doorway with shaking fingers. Nine hundred feet beneath him rolled the icy waters of the Atlantic. Werner gulped. He'd been the one to ask for this tour. He couldn't back out now.

Werner took a deep breath before he uncurled his fingers and stepped down the ladder that linked the engine car to the airship. Now nothing stood between him and the open sea below. The wind raced past him at nearly eighty miles an hour, and he had to hook his elbow around the ladder's railing to keep from being blown off. Below him, Kollmer casually swung himself into the car where he greeted the mechanic on duty tending the engine. Neither one of them seemed disturbed by the ear-popping roar of the machinery or the twenty-foot-long propeller whirling furiously just a few feet away. Inside the *Hindenburg* Werner felt like he was riding on a cloud. But this was like being shot through the sky in a bullet.

Irene was glad she'd changed into her best dress. The dining room looked so elegant. Gleaming china edged with the Zeppelin Company logo was carefully arranged on crisp white tablecloths and a vase of fresh flowers sat in the center of every table. Uniformed stewards moved from guest to guest, serving drinks and taking orders. It was exactly like being at a fine restaurant — all that was missing were the candles.

While her parents selected a bottle of wine from the long list, Irene studied the menu. It was hard to choose between the sole and the venison, but she finally settled on the sole. It seemed more sophisticated. When the steward stood by the table with a serving tray and offered her the first of three courses, Irene felt as glamorous as an American movie star. She hoped no one would notice that her brothers were making hats out of their huge linen napkins.

Irene's mother, who was usually seasick on long ocean voyages, hadn't complained about her stomach once. She had even requested a second serving of soup. Her father was cheerful and rested after a long afternoon nap in the lounge. He looked like he'd been on a two-week vacation. Mr. Doehner lifted his glass and toasted the giant zeppelin, "Here's to the *Hindenburg*, the only way to fly."

(Above) A meal aboard the *Hindenburg* was like a visit to an exclusive restaurant, complete with its own wine list (left). The chief cook and his five assistants prepared three meals a day, plus afternoon tea, for up to 100 people (below and bottom). On a typical voyage, the *Hindenburg*'s passengers and crew ate their way through 440 pounds of potatoes, 800 eggs, and 220 pounds of butter and cheese. The officers dined in their own mess, to the right of the kitchen, while the crew shared meals in the mess on its left, where Werner sets the tables. A miniature elevator delivered food from the kitchen to a serving pantry on A-deck. Stewards then brought the meals to the dining room. Irene and her family are served at far right.

Disaster

May 6, 1937

The *Hindenburg* had flown into the wind all the way across the Atlantic and now thunderstorms prevented it from landing at the airfield in Lakehurst, New Jersey. To pass the time until it was calm enough to land, Captain Pruss took his passengers on an airborne tour of the East Coast of America. Irene hadn't expected to see New York, but suddenly there it was, right below her — the most exciting city in the world.

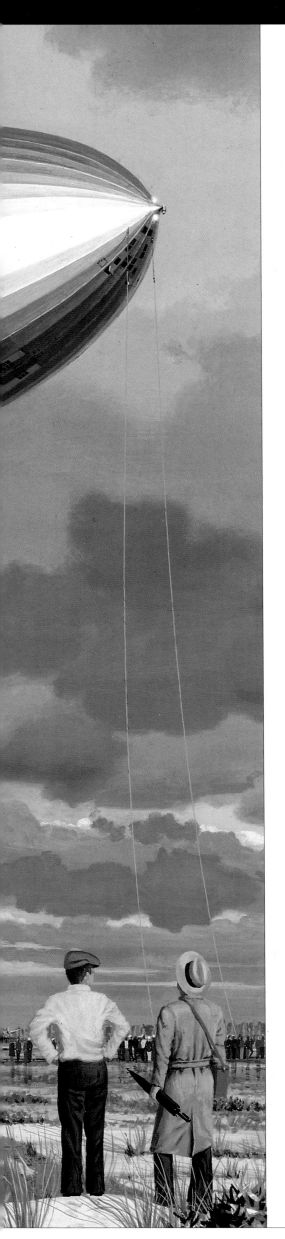

While waiting for the weather to clear, the *Hindenburg* cruised over Boston, New York, and the shores of New Jersey (above). One passenger reported that while the sight of a giant airship scattered dogs, chickens, and pigs, cows and sheep did not appear to notice it at all.

(Above) One of the last photos taken from the *Hindenburg*. Moments before the disaster, a passenger took this snapshot of the white-hatted landing crew waiting to catch the ropes about to be dropped from the airship. (Left) The *Hindenburg* hovers over the landing field in the last moments of its life.

Beneath the giant zeppelin, the tops of the skyscrapers poked up like nails. When they passed over the harbor, the Statue of Liberty seemed as tiny as a souvenir figurine. Small planes dipped their wings in greeting as they buzzed past. Walter leaned so far out the window to wave back at them that Irene had to grab the back of his shirt to keep him from falling. A chorus of honking car horns drifted up to greet the *Hindenburg* as it floated over the island of Manhattan all the way to the Empire State Building. The zeppelin flew so close to it that Irene could see the expressions of the tourists on the observation deck as they gaped and pointed, and the panting photographers brandishing their cameras as they rushed to the top of the building for a better shot. Even from the air, she could feel the city humming with life.

By 7:00 P.M. the surprise tour was long over and the *Hindenburg* was more than twelve hours late for its scheduled landing at the airfield in Lakehurst. The zeppelin had already circled the field several times in the past hour, hoping for a break in the weather. Now it made a sharp turn and began to descend as it approached the mooring mast. Irene stood by a window watching the last few drops of rain fall as the landing site came into view once more.

Below her, the landing crew stood ready on the field, prepared to catch the ropes that would soon be thrown from the *Hindenburg*. It would take more than two hundred men to haul the huge zeppelin to the ground. Just like pulling a gigantic balloon from the sky, thought Irene. Suddenly, she heard her mother gasp. As she turned to see what was the matter, the floor dropped out from under her.

Down in the officers' mess, Werner was stacking clean dishes in the cupboard. Without warning, he was thrown against the wall. Saucers and glasses crashed and shattered around him. The floor was slanting at a crazy angle, as if the tail of the ship had fallen out of the air. What was going on? Werner dropped to his knees and crawled around the broken china toward the open door of the mess.

Irene felt herself falling, and then she heard an incredible roar. Flames exploded through the wall at the far end of the room. The floor began to tilt toward the fire and she was sliding backward, straight into it. She shredded the skin on her elbows and knees in a desperate scramble to keep from being rolled into the flames. Tables, chairs, suitcases, and bodies tumbled past her. Passengers screamed in terror and shoved each other out of the way to get as far as possible from the fire.

A choking wave of heat and smoke nearly knocked Werner over as he peered around the door frame. Flames were rushing up

the corridor from the tail end of the airship. Werner stumbled into the hall and began to crawl up the slanting passageway, away from the flames. But the smoke was so thick he could barely breathe. He was running out of air. He felt so tired. His legs were like lead. If only he could rest here awhile....

A loud "Boom!" sounded above his head and suddenly cold water streamed over him, soaking his face and his uniform. It woke him like a slap.

Werner shook the water from his eyes and looked behind him. The blaze was picking up speed. Orange flames were already curling around the doorway to the officers' mess where he'd stood just a moment before. He couldn't outrun the fire for long. He searched frantically for a way out. Then, just ahead, he saw the hatch in the floor used for loading provisions aboard the airship. In desperation, Werner kicked away the cover and dived through the opening.

Somehow in the smoke-filled tangle of screaming passengers and scattered furniture Irene found her mother. They grabbed each other's hands and struggled to stand up. Her mother's face was frantic. Where were the boys? Walter and Werner had been thrown together out of sight between the legs of an overturned table. They coughed and sobbed with fright. Blood streamed from Walter's nose.

Where the map of the world had decorated the side of the lounge, there was now a wall of flame. Soon the whole room would be ablaze. There was only one way out: through the windows. Irene looked at her mother. They both knew what they had to do. Each of them grabbed one of the squirming, choking boys and dragged him to an open window. They hoisted the brothers up to the windowsill

and, one after the other, pushed them out. First Werner fell, then Walter, his arms and legs flailing. Through the smoke, Irene thought she saw one of her brothers caught in the arms of a man on the ground. But she didn't have a chance to watch for the other. She could hear metal crashing around her as the zeppelin's frame began to collapse. Then the flames leapt forward, igniting her hair and the back of her dress. Just before the searing pain made her mind go black, Irene pulled herself to the top of the sill and jumped.

Werner Franz hit the ground with a thud. The sandy soil was burning hot. He struggled to his feet and clawed his way through a white-hot tangle of girders and wire as pieces of burning fabric rained around his head. They sizzled as they hit his dripping uniform. The fire roared in his ears. He knew he had to run for his life.

He ran blindly, his arms shielding his face, until the air cleared and he found himself at the edge of the landing field. Gasping for breath, Werner turned back to see the *Hindenburg* on the ground, aflame from end to end. An enormous column of fire shot out through its nose. Incredibly, members of the landing crew were running toward the burning airship in search of any survivors. Even more incredibly, Werner saw tiny figures stumbling out of the zeppelin and crawling away from the inferno to safety.

Through the smoke he saw a girl, her dress and hair on fire, launch herself from one of the lounge windows like an exotic, flaming bird. Werner had to look away before she landed. By the time he could bring himself to look back, a few members of the landing crew were carrying her smoking body across the sand. As Werner watched, what was left of the *Hindenburg* blazed like a gigantic paper lantern and crumpled to the earth.

(Above) An identification button like this one was issued to all members of the Lakehurst ground crew. (Opposite) As the flaming airship fell to the ground, desperate passengers began to leap from the windows. (Left) A survivor whose clothes have burned off is helped away from the wreck. (Right) A rare color photo shows a fire truck arriving too late to douse the flames that destroyed the **Hindenburg.**

1 The first burst of flame appeared near the tail of the airship and quickly spread forward.

2 As the hydrogen from the gas cells burned away, the zeppelin's stern dropped out of the sky.

3 In just thirty-four seconds, the giant airship crashed to the ground, completely aflame.

4 The bow of the burning zeppelin was the last section to hit the landing field. (Left) Once the airship was on the ground, two-thirds of the people aboard the *Hindenburg* managed to leap from the zeppelin and fight through the wall of flames to safety.

Epilogue

On May 6, 1937, radio announcer Herbert Morrison was on the scene at the Lakehurst airfield, ready to record his impressions of the *Hindenburg*'s first American landing of the year. As the airship came into view, he described its approach in a calm, professional tone, "Here it comes, ladies and gentlemen, and what a sight it is, a thrilling one, just a marvelous sight." Then, as he spoke, the zeppelin caught fire before his eyes.

Morrison had to fight to keep talking, his horrified voice breaking as he cried, "It is burning, bursting into flames and is falling.... Oh, the humanity and all the passengers...!" In an instant, what was supposed to have been a routine landing turned into one of the most famous disasters of the twentieth century.

Amazingly, sixty-three of the ninety-seven passengers and crew aboard the *Hindenburg* that day survived, including Werner Franz, who was soaked by a bursting water tank. Mechanic Richard Kollmer also made it out alive. But thirty-four others, and one member of the ground crew, died. Irene Doehner jumped from the flaming zeppelin and was carried away from the blaze by the landing crew. But by then it was already too late. She was on fire before she leapt and died of her burns in the hospital a few hours later. Her mother and her brothers were saved, but her father never made it out of the zeppelin.

After the *Hindenburg* disaster, Werner Franz returned to Germany on an ocean liner. He arrived on May 22, 1937 — his fifteenth birthday. Back home he got a job at a hotel and later married and had a son. Today he is retired, lives in a small town in the west of Germany, and enjoys working in his garden. Even now, he does not like to talk about the last moments of the *Hindenburg*.

The world was horrified by news of the catastrophe and after the explosion, hydrogen-filled airships like the *Hindenburg* were considered too dangerous to carry passengers. And just a few years after the *Hindenburg* disaster, new airplanes were built that could make non-stop flights across the ocean in less time than the zeppelins ever could. But never again would airborne passengers travel in as much luxury as they had aboard the *Hindenburg*.

No one has ever been able to explain for certain what caused the *Hindenburg* to explode. Some people think it was an accident — perhaps lightning caused the hydrogen to ignite. Others think it was sabotage — perhaps someone who hated the Nazis planted a bomb on the airship. (In fact, the world's fears about Hitler and the Nazi party proved to be correct. Two years after the disaster, Germany invaded Poland, which led to the start of the Second World War.)

What went wrong?

After the disaster, the German and American governments each sent a team of investigators to Lakehurst to try to discover what had started the fire. They couldn't find any evidence of a bomb or of sabotage and concluded that the explosion was an accident.

At the time, the investigators thought that one of the metal wires that held the zeppelin's giant gasbags in place could have snapped as the *Hindenburg* made a sharp turn over the airfield. The snapping wire might have torn a hole in the closest gas cell, releasing hydrogen gas into the air. The freed gas could then have mixed with oxygen and been ignited by static electricity.

Recently, however, some researchers have argued that the fuel for the fire might not have been hydrogen after all. They suspect it could have been dope — the silver liquid painted on the fabric outer cover of the zeppelin.

(Above) By the morning of May 7, 1937, all that remained of the once-mighty *Hindenburg* was a blackened skeleton. A ring of guards was posted around the wreck to prevent looting and to protect any possible evidence that might show how the fire started. A charred letter (opposite), sent from Holland to Germany and placed aboard the *Hindenburg* for delivery in America, was retrieved from the ashes and delivered to its final destination. Almost everything else that could remind us of the elegant age of airship travel simply burned away.

All anyone knows for sure is that in thirty-four seconds — the time it took the zeppelin to crash to the ground — the age of the great passenger airships had come to an end.

Today, the same company that built the *Hindenburg* is making plans for a new generation of giant airships with metal skeletons, filled with non-flammable helium gas, that could be used for passenger flights, cargo transport, scientific observation, and sightseeing excursions. These new zeppelins will produce little pollution, be quiet, safe, and energy efficient. One day, not long from now, giant airships might cross the skies once again.

Dope made the *Hindenburg*'s covering waterproof and shrank it so that it would fit more tightly around the zeppelin's frame. The dope was made of a substance like varnish mixed with aluminum powder: an explosive combination, very

similar to the recipe for the solid rocket fuel used in today's space shuttles.

According to this theory, the storm on the evening of May 6, 1937, might have left enough electricity in the air to produce an electric charge,

which could have ignited the zeppelin's highly flammable outer cover. If this theory is correct and the outer cover was actually what caught fire first, the *Hindenburg* would have burned that night whether it was filled with hydrogen or not.

Glossary

ballast: Water stored in tanks inside a zeppelin that could be dropped if the zeppelin needed to be made lighter. A lighter airship would rise more quickly or descend more slowly.

blimp: An airship that gets its shape from the lifting gas that fills it. Blimps have no internal frame and they will collapse like balloons if they are not inflated.

bow: The front of an airship.

catwalk: The narrow metal walkway extending the entire length of a zeppelin's frame. The keel catwalk allowed crewmembers to travel the full length of the bottom of the airship. The axial catwalk passed through the middle of the zeppelin and allowed crewmembers to reach the higher parts of the zeppelin's gas cells and framework.

dope: A liquid painted onto a zeppelin's fabric outer cover. Dope made the fabric waterproof, and stretched it more tightly over the airship's frame. The silver-colored aluminum particles in the *Hindenburg*'s dope also helped to reflect the sun's heat.

Duralumin: The lightweight metal used to construct the *Hindenburg*'s frame. The Duralumin framework was painted with a bright blue coating to make it corrosion-proof.

gangway: The stairs leading from the ground to the inside of a zeppelin.

hangar: A large building used for storing a zeppelin when it is not flying.

helium: The second lightest gas known. Helium is not flammable and is used to inflate today's blimps.

hydrogen: The lightest gas known. Hydrogen has greater lifting power than any other gas, but is extremely flammable.

landing field: The large, level area where an airship can land or take off.

lighter-than-air: A type of aircraft which relies on lifting gases like helium or hydrogen to keep it airborne. Heavier-than-air craft, like airplanes, need wings and engines to give them enough lift to remain in the sky.

mess: The room where the officers or crew of an airship eat their meals.

Nazi: A member of the political party that controlled Germany from 1933-1945. Adolf Hitler was the leader of this party.

promenade deck: The long narrow deck on an airship where passengers can go for walks.

propaganda: Ideas or information that are spread in order to encourage people to support a particular political party.

stern: The back of an airship.

swastika: A symbol used by the Nazi party. It is shaped like a cross with an arm attached to each section bending at right angles in a clockwise direction.

zeppelin: An airship that gets its shape from an internal frame. Inside the frame are gas cells filled with a lighter-than-air gas. Because of its frame, a zeppelin will keep its shape whether its gas cells are inflated or not. The zeppelin was invented in 1900 by Count Ferdinand von Zeppelin.

Photograph and Illustration Credits

Every effort has been made to correctly attribute all the material reproduced in this book. If any errors have unwittingly occurred, we will be happy to correct them in future editions.

All illustrations, unless otherwise designated, are by Ken Marschall © 2000.

Front cover: (Top left) Illustration by Donna Gordon
Front jacket flap: Corbis
Endpapers: Luggage sticker, Collection of Dennis Kromm
Page 7: Collection of Dennis Kromm
Page 8: (Right and top left) Ullstein; (Bottom left) Süddeutscher Verlag Bilderdienst
Page 9: (Left) National Air and Space Museum, Smithsonian Institution; (Right) Illustration by Jack McMaster
Page 10: Illustration by Donna Gordon
Page 11: Illustrations by Donna Gordon; (Top left) Corbis; (Bottom left) Collection of Dr. Douglas Robinson
Pages 12-15: Illustration by Donna Gordon
Page 16: (Left) National Air and Space Museum, Smithsonian Institution; (Bottom right) Luftschiffbau Zeppelin GmbH
Page 19: Ullstein
Page 20: (Left) Collection of Dennis Kromm; (Top right) Corbis; (Middle and bottom right) John Provan: Luftschiff Zeppelin Collection
Page 25: (All) John Provan: Luftschiff Zeppelin Collection
Page 27: (Top) Collection of Henry Jay Applegate; (Bottom left) Corbis; (Bottom right) International Museum of Photography at George Eastman House
Page 29: (All) Corbis
Page 30: Collection of Dennis Kromm
Page 31: Corbis

Recommended Further Reading

Hindenburg: An Illustrated History
Text by Rick Archbold, Paintings by Ken Marschall
(1994, Warner, U.S., Penguin, Canada; Orion, U.K.)
The splendidly illustrated story of lighter-than-air flight, featuring the triumphs and disasters of history's most famous airships.

The Disaster of the Hindenburg
By Shelley Tanaka (1993, Scholastic, U.S., Canada, U.K.)
Tells young readers the story of the great zeppelin's last flight.

The Golden Age of the Great Passenger Airships: Graf Zeppelin and Hindenburg
by Harold G. Dick with Douglas H. Robinson
(1985, Smithsonian Institution Press, U.S., U.K.)
A detailed technical examination of both of these notable airships.

Acknowledgments

I would like to thank long-time friend Dennis Kromm and German airship guru John Provan for their guidance and for sharing their vast photo and research collections; Dr. Wolfgang Meighörner, director of the Zeppelin Museum at Friedrichshafen, Germany, and his staff, for answering a myriad of difficult questions; Mireille Majoor and Hugh Brewster for their usual patience and accommodation of my perfectionism; Roland Hauser and Vern Shrock for their help and support throughout the project; and Laurie McGaw, whose marvelous skills have given these paintings life.
—Ken Marschall

For their invaluable support, inexhaustible supply of zeppelin knowledge, and unfailing good humor, I'd like to thank Dennis Kromm and John Provan. Thanks also to Hugh Brewster, Nan Froman, and Laurie Coulter for their expert assistance in sharpening the text. And warm thanks to Ken Marschall whose enormous talent makes the *Hindenburg* fly again in these pages.
—Mireille Majoor

For posing as models, I would like to thank: Marilyn, Daryl, Jennifer, Geoff, and Christina Logan, Arline and Gary Gorelle, Martin and Derek Warmelink, and Ross Phillips.
—Laurie McGaw

Paintings © 2000 Ken Marschall
Text, design and compilation © 2000
The Madison Press Limited

First published in 2000 by

Little, Brown and Company
3 Center Plaza
Boston, Massachusetts 02108
U.S.A.

1 3 5 7 9 10 8 6 4 2

**Library of Congress
Cataloging-in-Publication Data**

Majoor, Mireille
Inside the Hindenburg/
text by Mireille Majoor;
illustrated by Ken Marschall.
p. cm.
ISBN 0-316-12386-2
ISBN 0-316-12322-6
(Special Scholastic Edition)
1. Hindenburg (Airship) — Juvenile literature. 2. Aircraft accidents — New Jersey — Juvenile literature.
[1. Hindenburg (Airship) 2. Airships.
3. Aircraft accidents.]
I. Marschall, Ken, ill. II. Title.

TL659.H5 M35 2000
629.133'25—dc21

00-030157

Design, Typography and Art Direction: Gordon Sibley Design Inc.
Editorial Director: Hugh Brewster
Editorial Assistance: Susan Aihoshi
Additional Illustration: Laurie McGaw, Donna Gordon, Jack McMaster
Production Director: Susan Barrable
Production Coordinator: Donna Chong
Color Separation: Colour Technologies
Printing and Binding: Artegrafica S.p.A.

INSIDE THE HINDENBURG
was produced by
Madison Press Books,
which is under the direction of
Albert E. Cummings

**Produced by
Madison Press Books**
40 Madison Avenue
Toronto, Ontario
Canada M5R 2S1

Printed and bound in Italy